W9-CKI-318

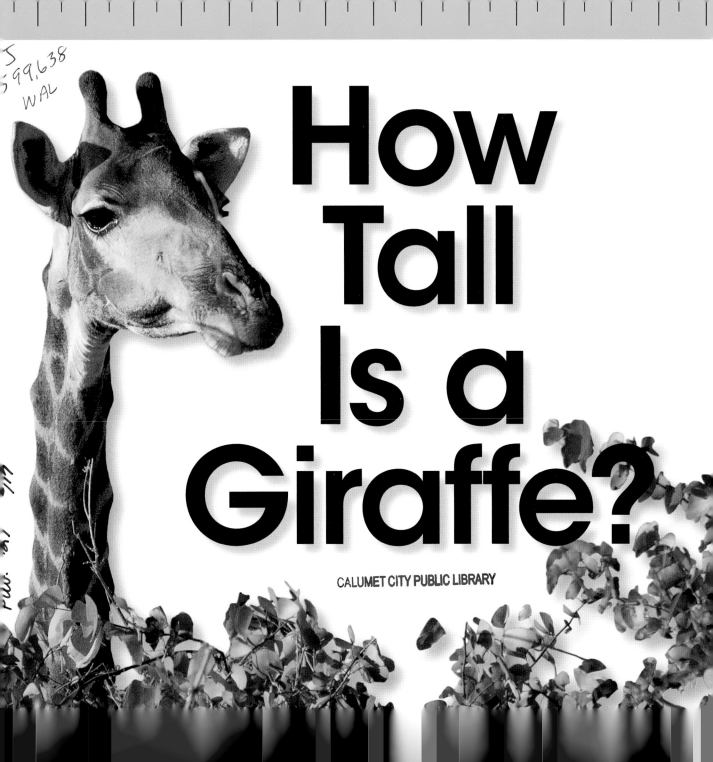

How
Tall
Is a
Giraffe?

The Child's World®
childsworld.com

Published by The Child's World®
1980 Lookout Drive • Mankato, MN 56003-1705
800-599-READ • www.childsworld.com

Photographs ©: Travel Stock/Shutterstock Images, cover,
1; Matthieu Gallet/Shutterstock Images, 2–3; Shutterstock
Images, 4, 10, 14, 14–15, 16, 18–19, 23; W. L. Davies/iStockphoto,
4–5; Hans Engbers/Shutterstock Images, 6–7; Vaclav Volrab/
Shutterstock Images, 9; Eric Isselee/Shutterstock Images, 10–11,
17; Anan Kaewkhammul/Shutterstock Images, 12–13; Amy
Nichole Harris/Shutterstock Images, 20–21

ISBN 9781503816824
LCCN 2016945664

Printed in the United States of America
PA02325

ABOUT THE AUTHOR

Kurt Waldendorf is a writer and editor.
He lives in Vermont with his wife and their
Old English sheepdog, Charlie.

NOTE FOR PARENTS AND TEACHERS

The Child's World® helps early readers develop their informational-reading skills by providing easy-to-read books that fascinate them and hold their interest. Encourage new readers by following these simple ideas:

BEFORE READING

- Page briefly through the book. Discuss the photos. What does the reader think he or she will learn in this book? Let the child ask questions.
- Look at the glossary together. Discuss the words.

READ THE BOOK

- Now read the book together, or let the child read the book independently.

AFTER READING

- Urge the child to think more. Ask questions such as, "What things are different among the animals shown in this book?"

A giraffe is the tallest land animal.
How tall is a giraffe?

A giraffe is born tall.
A **newborn** giraffe is
as tall as a doorway.

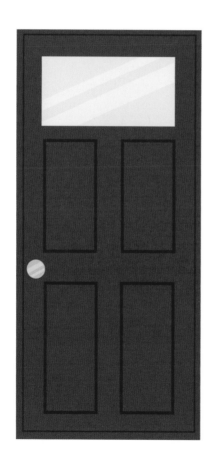

The giraffe grows taller. An adult giraffe would need to duck to walk under a bridge on a highway.

An elephant stands tall.
But it only reaches a
giraffe's shoulders.

A giraffe has long, skinny legs. Many people could walk under a giraffe without hitting their heads.

A giraffe has the longest neck of any animal. A giraffe's neck is 20 times longer than a human's neck.

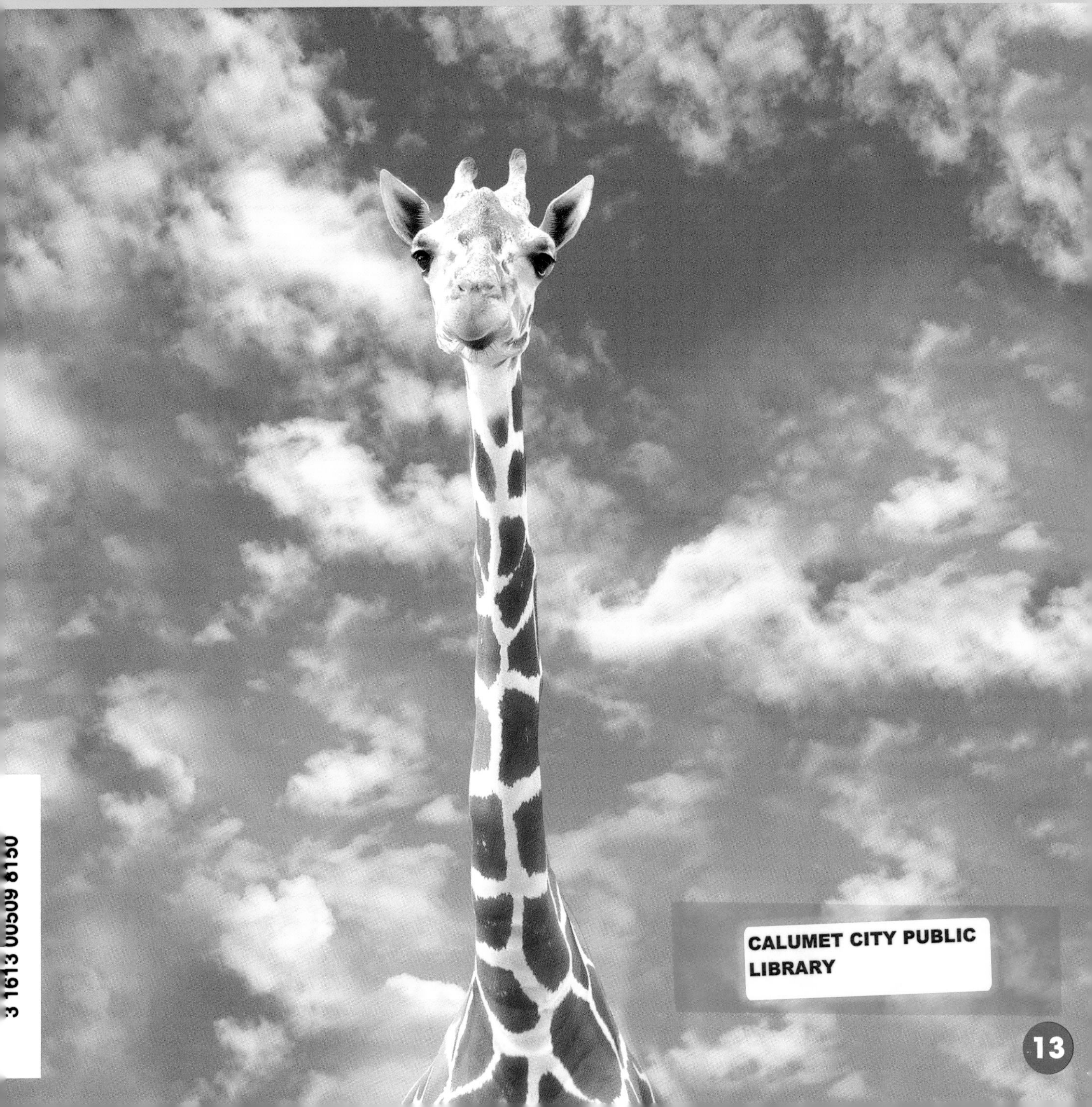

A giraffe needs a big heart to pump blood to its head. A giraffe's heart is the length of two 2-liter bottles.

A giraffe watches for **dangerous** lions.

A giraffe is as tall as five lions.

A giraffe grabs food from trees with its tongue. A giraffe's tongue is the length of an adult's **forearm** and hand.

A giraffe can reach
tree branches
the height of two
basketball hoops.
That is tall!

▶ A giraffe's height helps it to see danger coming from far away. This allows it to move before something dangerous gets too close.

▶ A giraffe has a hard time reaching down far enough to take a drink. It must spread its legs out wide in order to reach the ground with its head.

▶ A giraffe spends most of its day eating.

▶ A giraffe sleeps for only 30 minutes each day. It almost never lies down to sleep.

▶ No two giraffes have the same pattern of spots.

dangerous (DAYN-jur-uhs) Something is dangerous if it is likely to cause harm. A lion is dangerous to a giraffe. It can catch and eat a giraffe.

forearm (FOR-arm) A forearm is the part of a person's arm from the wrist to the elbow. A giraffe's tongue is longer than a person's forearm and hand.

newborn (NOO-born) Newborn means just recently having been born. Newborn giraffes stand up soon after they are born.

TO LEARN MORE

BOOKS

Loy, Jessica. *Weird & Wild Animal Facts*.
New York, NY: Henry Holt, 2015.

Marsh, Laura. *Giraffes*. Washington, DC:
National Geographic, 2016.

Smith, Lucy Sackett. *Giraffes: Towering Tall*.
New York, NY: PowerKids Press, 2010.

WEB SITES

Visit our Web site for links about giraffes:
childsworld.com/links

Note to Parents, Teachers, and Librarians: We routinely verify our Web links to make sure they are safe and active sites. So encourage your readers to check them out!

INDEX